Ayodele T. Awe

Confessions That Brings Prosperity.

Copyright 2012 by

Ayodele & Modupe Awe

All rights Reserved.

2012 Print.

www.taiyeaweministries.org

Email: taiye.awe@gmail.com

All scripture quotations are from the King James version, New King James Version and the New International Version of the Bible, except otherwise stated.

Genesis 27.28–29

King James Version (KJV)

[28]Therefore God give thee of the dew of heaven, and the fatness of the earth, and plenty of corn and wine:

[29]Let people serve thee, and nations bow down to thee: be lord over thy brethren, and let thy mother's sons bow down to thee: cursed be every one that curseth thee, and blessed be he that blesseth thee.

Genesis 27.28–29

New King James Version (NKJV)

[28] Therefore may God give you
Of the dew of heaven,
Of the fatness of the earth,
And plenty of grain and wine.
[29] Let peoples serve you,
And nations bow down to you.
Be master over your brethren,
And let your mother's sons bow down to you.
Cursed *be* everyone who curses you,
And blessed *be* those who bless you!"

Genesis 27.28–29 (NIV)

[28] May God give you heaven's dew
  and earth's richness—
  an abundance of grain and new wine.

²⁹ May nations serve you
and peoples bow down to you.
Be lord over your brothers,
and may the sons of your mother bow down to you.
May those who curse you be cursed
and those who bless you be blessed."

Genesis 27.39

King James Version (KJV)

³⁹And Isaac his father answered and said unto him, Behold, thy dwelling shall be the fatness of the earth, and of the dew of heaven from above;

Genesis 27.39 (New King James Version)

³⁹ Then Isaac his father answered and said to him:
" Behold, your dwelling shall be of the fatness of the earth,
And of the dew of heaven from above.

Genesis 27.39

New International Version (NIV)

³⁹ His father Isaac answered him,
"Your dwelling will be
away from the earth's richness,
away from the dew of heaven above.

Genesis 28:3-4

King James Version (KJV)

[3]And God Almighty bless thee, and make thee fruitful, and multiply thee, that thou mayest be a multitude of people;

[4]And give thee the blessing of Abraham, to thee, and to thy seed with thee; that thou mayest inherit the land wherein thou art a stranger, which God gave unto Abraham.

Genesis 28:3-4 (New King James Version)

[3] "May God Almighty bless you,
   And make you fruitful and multiply you,
   That you may be an assembly of peoples;

[4] And give you the blessing of Abraham,
   To you and your descendants with you,
   That you may inherit the land
   In which you are a stranger,
   Which God gave to Abraham."

Genesis 28:3-4

New International Version (NIV)

[3] May God Almighty bless you and make you fruitful and increase your numbers until you become a community of peoples. [4] May he give you and your descendants the blessing given to Abraham, so that you may take possession of the land where you now reside as a foreigner, the land God gave to Abraham."

Genesis 28.14

King James Version (KJV)

[14]And thy seed shall be as the dust of the earth, and thou shalt spread abroad to the west, and to the east, and to the north, and to the south: and in thee and in thy seed shall all the families of the earth be blessed.

Genesis 28.14 (New King James Version)

[14] Also your descendants shall be as the dust of the earth; you shall spread abroad to the west and the east, to the north and the south; and in you and in your seed all the families of the earth shall be blessed.

Genesis 28.14

New International Version (NIV)

[14] Your descendants will be like the dust of the earth, and you will spread out to the west and to the east, to the north and to the south. All peoples on earth will be blessed through you and your offspring.[

Genesis 28.15

King James Version (KJV)

[15]And, behold, I am with thee, and will keep thee in all places whither thou goest, and will bring thee again into this land; for I will not leave thee, until I have done that which I have spoken to thee of.

Genesis 28.15 (New King James Version)

[15] Behold, I *am* with you and will keep you wherever you go, and will bring you back to this land; for I will not leave you until I have done what I have spoken to you."

Genesis 28.15

New International Version (NIV)

[15] I am with you and will watch over you wherever you go, and I will bring you back to this land. I will not leave you until I have done what I have promised you."

Genesis 26.3

King James Version (KJV)

[3]Sojourn in this land, and I will be with thee, and will bless thee; for unto thee, and unto thy seed, I will give all these countries, and I will perform the oath which I sware unto Abraham thy father;

Genesis 26.3 (New King James Version)

[3] Dwell in this land, and I will be with you and bless you; for to you and your descendants I give all these lands, and I will perform the oath which I swore to Abraham your father.

Genesis 26.3

New International Version (NIV)

³ Stay in this land for a while, and I will be with you and will bless you. For to you and your descendants I will give all these lands and will confirm the oath I swore to your father Abraham.

Genesis 26:4

King James Version (KJV)

⁴And I will make thy seed to multiply as the stars of heaven, and will give unto thy seed all these countries; and in thy seed shall all the nations of the earth be blessed;

Genesis 26:4 (New King James Version)

⁴ And I will make your descendants multiply as the stars of heaven; I will give to your descendants all these lands; and in your seed all the nations of the earth shall be blessed;

Genesis 26:4

New International Version (NIV)

⁴ I will make your descendants as numerous as the stars in the sky and will give them all these lands, and through your offspring all nations on earth will be blessed,ᶦ

Genesis 26:12

King James Version (KJV)

¹²Then Isaac sowed in that land, and received in the same year an hundredfold: and the LORD blessed him.

Genesis 26.12 (New King James Version)

[12] Then Isaac sowed in that land, and reaped in the same year a hundredfold; and the LORD blessed him.

Genesis 26.12

New International Version (NIV)

[12] Isaac planted crops in that land and the same year reaped a hundredfold, because the LORD blessed him.

Amos 9.13

King James Version (KJV)

[13]Behold, the days come, saith the LORD, that the plowman shall overtake the reaper, and the treader of grapes him that soweth seed; and the mountains shall drop sweet wine, and all the hills shall melt.

Amos 9.13 (New King James Version)

[13] " Behold, the days are coming," says the LORD,
   " When the plowman shall overtake the reaper,
    And the treader of grapes him who sows seed;
    The mountains shall drip with sweet wine,
    And all the hills shall flow *with it.*

Amos 9.13

New International Version (NIV)

[13] "The days are coming," declares the LORD,

"when the reaper will be overtaken by the plowman
and the planter by the one treading grapes.
New wine will drip from the mountains
and flow from all the hills,

Deuteronomy 1.8

King James Version (KJV)

[8]Behold, I have set the land before you: go in and possess the land
which the LORD sware unto your fathers, Abraham, Isaac, and Jacob,
to give unto them and to their seed after them.

Deuteronomy 1.8

New King James Version (NKJV)

[8] See, I have set the land before you; go in and possess the land
which the LORD swore to your fathers—to Abraham, Isaac, and
Jacob—to give to them and their descendants after them.'

Deuteronomy 1.8

New International Version (NIV)

[8] See, I have given you this land. Go in and take possession of the land the LORD swore he would give to your fathers—to Abraham, Isaac and Jacob—and to their descendants after them."

Deuteronomy 1.11

King James Version (KJV)

[11](The LORD God of your fathers make you a thousand times so many more as ye are, and bless you, as he hath promised you!)

Deuteronomy 1.11

New King James Version (NKJV)

[11] May the LORD God of your fathers make you a thousand times more numerous than you are, and bless you as He has promised you!

Deuteronomy 1.11

New International Version (NIV)

[11] May the LORD, the God of your ancestors, increase you a thousand times and bless you as he has promised!

Deuteronomy 1.21

King James Version (KJV)

[21]Behold, the LORD thy God hath set the land before thee: go up and possess it, as the LORD God of thy fathers hath said unto thee; fear not, neither be discouraged.

Deuteronomy 1.21

New King James Version (NKJV)

[21] Look, the LORD your God has set the land before you; go up *and* possess *it*, as the LORD God of your fathers has spoken to you; do not fear or be discouraged.'

New International Version (NIV)

[21] See, the LORD your God has given you the land. Go up and take possession of it as the LORD, the God of your ancestors, told you. Do not be afraid; do not be discouraged."

Deuteronomy 2.25

King James Version (KJV)

[25]This day will I begin to put the dread of thee and the fear of thee upon the nations that are under the whole heaven, who shall hear report of thee, and shall tremble, and be in anguish because of thee.

Deuteronomy 2.25

New King James Version (NKJV)

[25] This day I will begin to put the dread and fear of you upon the nations under the whole heaven, who shall hear the report of you, and shall tremble and be in anguish because of you.'

Deuteronomy 2.25

New International Version (NIV)

[25] This very day I will begin to put the terror and fear of you on all the nations under heaven. They will hear reports of you and will tremble and be in anguish because of you."

Deuteronomy 2.31

King James Version (KJV)

[31] And the LORD said unto me, Behold, I have begun to give Sihon and his land before thee: begin to possess, that thou mayest inherit his land.

New King James Version (NKJV)

[31] "And the LORD said to me, 'See, I have begun to give Sihon and his land over to you. Begin to possess *it*, that you may inherit his land.'

New International Version (NIV)

^{31} The LORD said to me, "See, I have begun to deliver Sihon and his country over to you. Now begin to conquer and possess his land."

Deuteronomy 2.24

King James Version (KJV)

^{24}Rise ye up, take your journey, and pass over the river Arnon: behold, I have given into thine hand Sihon the Amorite, king of Heshbon, and his land: begin to possess it, and contend with him in battle.

New King James Version (NKJV)

^{24} "'Rise, take your journey, and cross over the River Arnon. Look, I have given into your hand Sihon the Amorite, king of Heshbon, and his land. Begin to possess *it*, and engage him in battle.

Deuteronomy 2.24

New International Version (NIV)

^{24} "Set out now and cross the Arnon Gorge. See, I have given into your hand Sihon the Amorite, king of Heshbon, and his country. Begin to take possession of it and engage him in battle.

Deuteronomy 4:37–40

King James Version (KJV)

[37]And because he loved thy fathers, therefore he chose their seed after them, and brought thee out in his sight with his mighty power out of Egypt;

[38]To drive out nations from before thee greater and mightier than thou art, to bring thee in, to give thee their land for an inheritance, as it is this day.

[39]Know therefore this day, and consider it in thine heart, that the LORD he is God in heaven above, and upon the earth beneath: there is none else.

[40]Thou shalt keep therefore his statutes, and his commandments, which I command thee this day, that it may go well with thee, and with thy children after thee, and that thou mayest prolong thy days upon the earth, which the LORD thy God giveth thee, for ever.

New King James Version (NKJV)

[37] And because He loved your fathers, therefore He chose their descendants after them; and He brought you out of Egypt with His Presence, with His mighty power, [38] driving out from before you nations greater and mightier than you, to bring you in, to give you their land *as* an inheritance, as *it is* this day. [39] Therefore know this day, and consider *it* in your heart, that the LORD Himself *is* God in heaven above and on the earth beneath; *there is* no other. [40] You shall therefore keep His statutes and His commandments which I

command you today, that it may go well with you and with your children after you, and that you may prolong *your* days in the land which the LORD your God is giving you for all time."

Deuteronomy 4:37-40

New International Version (NIV)

[37] Because he loved your ancestors and chose their descendants after them, he brought you out of Egypt by his Presence and his great strength, [38] to drive out before you nations greater and stronger than you and to bring you into their land to give it to you for your inheritance, as it is today.

[39] Acknowledge and take to heart this day that the LORD is God in heaven above and on the earth below. There is no other. [40] Keep his decrees and commands, which I am giving you today, so that it may go well with you and your children after you and that you may live long in the land the LORD your God gives you for all time.

Deuteronomy 5:33

King James Version (KJV)

[33]Ye shall walk in all the ways which the LORD your God hath commanded you, that ye may live, and that it may be well with you, and that ye may prolong your days in the land which ye shall possess.

New King James Version (NKJV)

[33] You shall walk in all the ways which the LORD your God has commanded you, that you may live and *that it may be* well with you, and *that* you may prolong *your* days in the land which you shall possess.

New International Version (NIV)

[33] Walk in obedience to all that the LORD your God has commanded you, so that you may live and prosper and prolong your days in the land that you will possess.

Deuteronomy 6:3

King James Version (KJV)

[3]Hear therefore, O Israel, and observe to do it; that it may be well with thee, and that ye may increase mightily, as the LORD God of thy fathers hath promised thee, in the land that floweth with milk and honey.

New King James Version (NKJV)

[3] Therefore hear, O Israel, and be careful to observe *it,* that it may be well with you, and that you may multiply greatly as the LORD God of your fathers has promised you—'a land flowing with milk and honey.'

New International Version (NIV)

³ Hear, Israel, and be careful to obey so that it may go well with you and that you may increase greatly in a land flowing with milk and honey, just as the LORD, the God of your ancestors, promised you.

Deuteronomy 6:6-9

King James Version (KJV)

⁶And these words, which I command thee this day, shall be in thine heart:

⁷And thou shalt teach them diligently unto thy children, and shalt talk of them when thou sittest in thine house, and when thou walkest by the way, and when thou liest down, and when thou risest up.

⁸And thou shalt bind them for a sign upon thine hand, and they shall be as frontlets between thine eyes.

⁹And thou shalt write them upon the posts of thy house, and on thy gates.

New King James Version (NKJV)

⁶ "And these words which I command you today shall be in your heart. ⁷ You shall teach them diligently to your children, and shall talk of them when you sit in your house, when you walk by the way, when you lie down, and when you rise up. ⁸ You shall bind them as a sign on your hand, and they shall be as frontlets between your eyes. ⁹ You shall write them on the doorposts of your house and on your gates.

New International Version (NIV)

[6] These commandments that I give you today are to be on your hearts. [7] Impress them on your children. Talk about them when you sit at home and when you walk along the road, when you lie down and when you get up. [8] Tie them as symbols on your hands and bind them on your foreheads. [9] Write them on the doorframes of your houses and on your gates.

Deuteronomy 6:10-11

King James Version (KJV)

[10]And it shall be, when the LORD thy God shall have brought thee into the land which he sware unto thy fathers, to Abraham, to Isaac, and to Jacob, to give thee great and goodly cities, which thou buildedst not,

[11]And houses full of all good things, which thou filledst not, and wells digged, which thou diggedst not, vineyards and olive trees, which thou plantedst not; when thou shalt have eaten and be full;

New King James Version (NKJV)

Caution Against Disobedience

[10] "So it shall be, when the LORD your God brings you into the land of which He swore to your fathers, to Abraham, Isaac, and Jacob, to give you large and beautiful cities which you did not build, [11] houses full of all good things, which you did not fill, hewn-out wells which you did not dig, vineyards and olive trees which you did not plant—when you have eaten and are full—

New International Version (NIV)

[10] When the LORD your God brings you into the land he swore to your fathers, to Abraham, Isaac and Jacob, to give you—a land with large, flourishing cities you did not build, [11] houses filled with all kinds of good things you did not provide, wells you did not dig, and vineyards and olive groves you did not plant—then when you eat and are satisfied,

Deuteronomy 7.6

King James Version (KJV)

[6]For thou art an holy people unto the LORD thy God: the LORD thy God hath chosen thee to be a special people unto himself, above all people that are upon the face of the earth.

New King James Version (NKJV)

[6] "For you *are* a holy people to the LORD your God; the LORD your God has chosen you to be a people for Himself, a special treasure above all the peoples on the face of the earth.

New International Version (NIV)

[6] For you are a people holy to the LORD your God. The LORD your God has chosen you out of all the peoples on the face of the earth to be his people, his treasured possession.

Deuteronomy 7.9

King James Version (KJV)

[9]Know therefore that the LORD thy God, he is God, the faithful God, which keepeth covenant and mercy with them that love him and keep his commandments to a thousand generations;

New King James Version (NKJV)

[9] "Therefore know that the LORD your God, He *is* God, the faithful God who keeps covenant and mercy for a thousand generations with those who love Him and keep His commandments;

New International Version (NIV)

[9] Know therefore that the LORD your God is God; he is the faithful God, keeping his covenant of love to a thousand generations of those who love him and keep his commandments.

Deuteronomy 7.12-13

King James Version (KJV)

[12]Wherefore it shall come to pass, if ye hearken to these judgments, and keep, and do them, that the LORD thy God shall keep unto thee the covenant and the mercy which he sware unto thy fathers:

[13]And he will love thee, and bless thee, and multiply thee: he will also bless the fruit of thy womb, and the fruit of thy land, thy corn, and thy wine, and thine oil, the increase of thy kine, and the flocks of thy sheep, in the land which he sware unto thy fathers to give thee.

New King James Version (NKJV)

Blessings of Obedience

[12] "Then it shall come to pass, because you listen to these judgments, and keep and do them, that the LORD your God will keep with you the covenant and the mercy which He swore to your fathers. [13] And He will love you and bless you and multiply you; He will also bless the fruit of your womb and the fruit of your land, your grain and your new wine and your oil, the increase of your cattle and the offspring of your flock, in the land of which He swore to your fathers to give you.

New International Version (NIV)

[12] If you pay attention to these laws and are careful to follow them, then the LORD your God will keep his covenant of love with you, as he swore to your ancestors. [13] He will love you and bless you and increase your numbers. He will bless the fruit of your womb, the crops of your land—your grain, new wine and olive oil—the calves of your herds and the lambs of your flocks in the land he swore to your ancestors to give you.

Deuteronomy 8:1

King James Version (KJV)

Deuteronomy 8

[1]All the commandments which I command thee this day shall ye observe to do, that ye may live, and multiply, and go in and possess the land which the LORD sware unto your fathers.

New King James Version (NKJV)

Remember the LORD Your God

[1] "Every commandment which I command you today you must be careful to observe, that you may live and multiply, and go in and possess the land of which the LORD swore to your fathers.

New International Version (NIV)

Deuteronomy 8

Do Not Forget the LORD

[1] Be careful to follow every command I am giving you today, so that you may live and increase and may enter and possess the land the LORD promised on oath to your ancestors.

Deuteronomy 8:7-10

King James Version (KJV)

[7] For the LORD thy God bringeth thee into a good land, a land of brooks of water, of fountains and depths that spring out of valleys and hills;

[8] A land of wheat, and barley, and vines, and fig trees, and pomegranates; a land of oil olive, and honey;

[9] A land wherein thou shalt eat bread without scarceness, thou shalt not lack any thing in it; a land whose stones are iron, and out of whose hills thou mayest dig brass.

[10]When thou hast eaten and art full, then thou shalt bless the LORD thy God for the good land which he hath given thee.

New King James Version (NKJV)

[7] For the LORD your God is bringing you into a good land, a land of brooks of water, of fountains and springs, that flow out of valleys and hills; [8] a land of wheat and barley, of vines and fig trees and pomegranates, a land of olive oil and honey; [9] a land in which you will eat bread without scarcity, in which you will lack nothing; a land whose stones *are* iron and out of whose hills you can dig copper. [10] When you have eaten and are full, then you shall bless the LORD your God for the good land which He has given you.

New International Version (NIV)

[7] For the LORD your God is bringing you into a good land—a land with brooks, streams, and deep springs gushing out into the valleys and hills; [8] a land with wheat and barley, vines and fig trees, pomegranates, olive oil and honey; [9] a land where bread will not be scarce and you will lack nothing; a land where the rocks are iron and you can dig copper out of the hills.

[10] When you have eaten and are satisfied, praise the LORD your God for the good land he has given you.

Deuteronomy 8.12-13

King James Version (KJV)

[12]Lest when thou hast eaten and art full, and hast built goodly houses, and dwelt therein;

[13]And when thy herds and thy flocks multiply, and thy silver and thy gold is multiplied, and all that thou hast is multiplied;

New King James Version (NKJV)

[12] lest—*when* you have eaten and are full, and have built beautiful houses and dwell *in them;* [13] and *when* your herds and your flocks multiply, and your silver and your gold are multiplied, and all that you have is multiplied;

New International Version (NIV)

[12] Otherwise, when you eat and are satisfied, when you build fine houses and settle down, [13] and when your herds and flocks grow large and your silver and gold increase and all you have is multiplied,

Deuteronomy 8.18

King James Version (KJV)

[18]But thou shalt remember the LORD thy God: for it is he that giveth thee power to get wealth, that he may establish his covenant which he sware unto thy fathers, as it is this day.

New King James Version (NKJV)

¹⁸ "And you shall remember the LORD your God, for *it is* He who gives you power to get wealth, that He may establish His covenant which He swore to your fathers, as *it is* this day.

New International Version (NIV)

¹⁸ But remember the LORD your God, for it is he who gives you the ability to produce wealth, and so confirms his covenant, which he swore to your ancestors, as it is today.

Deuteronomy 9:1

King James Version (KJV)

Deuteronomy 9

¹Hear, O Israel: Thou art to pass over Jordan this day, to go in to possess nations greater and mightier than thyself, cities great and fenced up to heaven,

Deuteronomy 9:1

New King James Version (NKJV)

¹ "Hear, O Israel: You *are* to cross over the Jordan today, and go in to dispossess nations greater and mightier than yourself, cities great and fortified up to heaven.

New International Version (NIV)

Deuteronomy 9

Not Because of Israel's Righteousness

¹ Hear, Israel: You are now about to cross the Jordan to go in and dispossess nations greater and stronger than you, with large cities that have walls up to the sky.

Deuteronomy 10:11

King James Version (KJV)

¹¹And the LORD said unto me, Arise, take thy journey before the people, that they may go in and possess the land, which I sware unto their fathers to give unto them.

New King James Version (NKJV)

¹¹ Then the LORD said to me, 'Arise, begin *your* journey before the people, that they may go in and possess the land which I swore to their fathers to give them.'

New International Version (NIV)

¹¹ "Go," the LORD said to me, "and lead the people on their way, so that they may enter and possess the land I swore to their ancestors to give them."

Deuteronomy 10:20–21

King James Version (KJV)

[20]Thou shalt fear the LORD thy God; him shalt thou serve, and to him shalt thou cleave, and swear by his name.

[21]He is thy praise, and he is thy God, that hath done for thee these great and terrible things, which thine eyes have seen.

New King James Version (NKJV)

[20] You shall fear the LORD your God; you shall serve Him, and to Him you shall hold fast, and take oaths in His name. [21] He *is* your praise, and He *is* your God, who has done for you these great and awesome things which your eyes have seen.

New International Version (NIV)

[20] Fear the LORD your God and serve him. Hold fast to him and take your oaths in his name. [21] He is the one you praise; he is your God, who performed for you those great and awesome wonders you saw with your own eyes.

Deuteronomy 11:8–10

King James Version (KJV)

[8]Therefore shall ye keep all the commandments which I command you this day, that ye may be strong, and go in and possess the land, whither ye go to possess it;

[9]And that ye may prolong your days in the land, which the LORD sware unto your fathers to give unto them and to their seed, a land that floweth with milk and honey.

[10]For the land, whither thou goest in to possess it, is not as the land of Egypt, from whence ye came out, where thou sowedst thy seed, and wateredst it with thy foot, as a garden of herbs:

New King James Version (NKJV)

[8] "Therefore you shall keep every commandment which I command you today, that you may be strong, and go in and possess the land which you cross over to possess, [9] and that you may prolong *your* days in the land which the LORD swore to give your fathers, to them and their descendants, 'a land flowing with milk and honey.'[a] [10] For the land which you go to possess *is* not like the land of Egypt from which you have come, where you sowed your seed and watered *it* by foot, as a vegetable garden;

New International Version (NIV)

[8] Observe therefore all the commands I am giving you today, so that you may have the strength to go in and take over the land that you are crossing the Jordan to possess, [9] and so that you may live long in the land the LORD swore to your ancestors to give to them and their descendants, a land flowing with milk and honey. [10] The land you are entering to take over is not like the land of Egypt, from which you have come, where you planted your seed and irrigated it by foot as in a vegetable garden.

Deuteronomy 11.11-13

King James Version (KJV)

[11]But the land, whither ye go to possess it, is a land of hills and valleys, and drinketh water of the rain of heaven:

[12]A land which the LORD thy God careth for: the eyes of the LORD thy God are always upon it, from the beginning of the year even unto the end of the year.

[13]And it shall come to pass, if ye shall hearken diligently unto my commandments which I command you this day, to love the LORD your God, and to serve him with all your heart and with all your soul,

New King James Version (NKJV)

[11] but the land which you cross over to possess *is* a land of hills and valleys, which drinks water from the rain of heaven, [12] a land for which the LORD your God cares; the eyes of the LORD your God *are* always on it, from the beginning of the year to the very end of the year.

[13] 'And it shall be that if you earnestly obey My commandments which I command you today, to love the LORD your God and serve Him with all your heart and with all your soul,

New International Version (NIV)

[11] But the land you are crossing the Jordan to take possession of is a land of mountains and valleys that drinks rain from heaven. [12] It is a

land the LORD your God cares for; the eyes of the LORD your God are continually on it from the beginning of the year to its end.

13 So if you faithfully obey the commands I am giving you today—to love the LORD your God and to serve him with all your heart and with all your soul—

Deuteronomy 11.14-15

King James Version (KJV)

14That I will give you the rain of your land in his due season, the first rain and the latter rain, that thou mayest gather in thy corn, and thy wine, and thine oil.

15And I will send grass in thy fields for thy cattle, that thou mayest eat and be full.

New King James Version (NKJV)

14 then I will give *you* the rain for your land in its season, the early rain and the latter rain, that you may gather in your grain, your new wine, and your oil. 15 And I will send grass in your fields for your livestock, that you may eat and be filled.

New International Version (NIV)

14 then I will send rain on your land in its season, both autumn and spring rains, so that you may gather in your grain, new wine and olive oil. 15 I will provide grass in the fields for your cattle, and you will eat and be satisfied.

Deuteronomy 11.18–19

King James Version (KJV)

[18]Therefore shall ye lay up these my words in your heart and in your soul, and bind them for a sign upon your hand, that they may be as frontlets between your eyes.

[19]And ye shall teach them your children, speaking of them when thou sittest in thine house, and when thou walkest by the way, when thou liest down, and when thou risest up.

New King James Version (NKJV)

[18] "Therefore you shall lay up these words of mine in your heart and in your soul, and bind them as a sign on your hand, and they shall be as frontlets between your eyes. [19] You shall teach them to your children, speaking of them when you sit in your house, when you walk by the way, when you lie down, and when you rise up.

New International Version (NIV)

[18] Fix these words of mine in your hearts and minds; tie them as symbols on your hands and bind them on your foreheads. [19] Teach them to your children, talking about them when you sit at home and when you walk along the road, when you lie down and when you get up.

Deuteronomy 11.20-24

King James Version (KJV)

[20]And thou shalt write them upon the door posts of thine house, and upon thy gates:

[21]That your days may be multiplied, and the days of your children, in the land which the LORD sware unto your fathers to give them, as the days of heaven upon the earth.

[22]For if ye shall diligently keep all these commandments which I command you, to do them, to love the LORD your God, to walk in all his ways, and to cleave unto him;

[23]Then will the LORD drive out all these nations from before you, and ye shall possess greater nations and mightier than yourselves.

[24]Every place whereon the soles of your feet shall tread shall be yours: from the wilderness and Lebanon, from the river, the river Euphrates, even unto the uttermost sea shall your coast be.

New King James Version (NKJV)

[20] And you shall write them on the doorposts of your house and on your gates, [21] that your days and the days of your children may be multiplied in the land of which the LORD swore to your fathers to give them, like the days of the heavens above the earth.

[22] "For if you carefully keep all these commandments which I command you to do—to love the LORD your God, to walk in all His ways, and to hold fast to Him— [23] then the LORD will drive out all

these nations from before you, and you will dispossess greater and mightier nations than yourselves. [24] Every place on which the sole of your foot treads shall be yours: from the wilderness and Lebanon, from the river, the River Euphrates, even to the Western Sea,[a] shall be your territory.

New International Version (NIV)

[20] Write them on the doorframes of your houses and on your gates, [21] so that your days and the days of your children may be many in the land the LORD swore to give your ancestors, as many as the days that the heavens are above the earth.

[22] If you carefully observe all these commands I am giving you to follow—to love the LORD your God, to walk in obedience to him and to hold fast to him— [23] then the LORD will drive out all these nations before you, and you will dispossess nations larger and stronger than you. [24] Every place where you set your foot will be yours: Your territory will extend from the desert to Lebanon, and from the Euphrates River to the Mediterranean Sea.

Deuteronomy 11:25-27

King James Version (KJV)

[25]There shall no man be able to stand before you: for the LORD your God shall lay the fear of you and the dread of you upon all the land that ye shall tread upon, as he hath said unto you.

[26]Behold, I set before you this day a blessing and a curse;

[27]A blessing, if ye obey the commandments of the LORD your God, which I command you this day.

New King James Version (NKJV)

[25] No man shall be able to stand against you; the LORD your God will put the dread of you and the fear of you upon all the land where you tread, just as He has said to you.

[26] "Behold, I set before you today a blessing and a curse: [27] the blessing, if you obey the commandments of the LORD your God which I command you today;

New International Version (NIV)

[25] No one will be able to stand against you. The LORD your God, as he promised you, will put the terror and fear of you on the whole land, wherever you go.

[26] See, I am setting before you today a blessing and a curse— [27] the blessing if you obey the commands of the LORD your God that I am giving you today;

Deuteronomy 12.11

King James Version (KJV)

[11]Then there shall be a place which the LORD your God shall choose to cause his name to dwell there; thither shall ye bring all that I command you; your burnt offerings, and your sacrifices, your tithes, and the heave offering of your hand, and all your choice vows which ye vow unto the LORD.

New King James Version (NKJV)

[11] then there will be the place where the LORD your God chooses to make His name abide. There you shall bring all that I command you: your burnt offerings, your sacrifices, your tithes, tNew International Version (NIV)

[11] Then to the place the LORD your God will choose as a dwelling for his Name—there you are to bring everything I command you: your burnt offerings and sacrifices, your tithes and special gifts, and all the choice possessions you have vowed to the LORD.

he heave offerings of your hand, and all your choice offerings which you vow to the LORD.

Deuteronomy 13:4

King James Version (KJV)

[4]Ye shall walk after the LORD your God, and fear him, and keep his commandments, and obey his voice, and ye shall serve him, and cleave unto him.

New King James Version (NKJV)

[4] You shall walk after the LORD your God and fear Him, and keep His commandments and obey His voice; you shall serve Him and hold fast to Him.

New International Version (NIV)

[4] It is the LORD your God you must follow, and him you must revere. Keep his commands and obey him; serve him and hold fast to him.

Deuteronomy 14.2

King James Version (KJV)

[2]For thou art an holy people unto the LORD thy God, and the LORD hath chosen thee to be a peculiar people unto himself, above all the nations that are upon the earth.

New King James Version (NKJV)

[2] For you *are* a holy people to the LORD your God, and the LORD has chosen you to be a people for Himself, a special treasure above all the peoples who *are* on the face of the earth.

New International Version (NIV)

[2] for you are a people holy to the LORD your God. Out of all the peoples on the face of the earth, the LORD has chosen you to be his treasured possession.

Deuteronomy 14.22

King James Version (KJV)

[22]Thou shalt truly tithe all the increase of thy seed, that the field bringeth forth year by year.

New King James Version (NKJV)

[22] "You shall truly tithe all the increase of your grain that the field produces year by year.

New International Version (NIV)

Tithes

[22] Be sure to set aside a tenth of all that your fields produce each year.

Deuteronomy 15:4

King James Version (KJV)

[4]Save when there shall be no poor among you; for the LORD shall greatly bless thee in the land which the LORD thy God giveth thee for an inheritance to possess it:

New King James Version (NKJV)

[4] except when there may be no poor among you; for the LORD will greatly bless you in the land which the LORD your God is giving you to possess *as* an inheritance—

New International Version (NIV)

[4] However, there need be no poor people among you, for in the land the LORD your God is giving you to possess as your inheritance, he will richly bless you,

Deuteronomy 15:6

King James Version (KJV)

[6]For the LORD thy God blesseth thee, as he promised thee: and thou shalt lend unto many nations, but thou shalt not borrow; and thou shalt reign over many nations, but they shall not reign over thee.

New King James Version (NKJV)

[6] For the LORD your God will bless you just as He promised you; you shall lend to many nations, but you shall not borrow; you shall reign over many nations, but they shall not reign over you.

New International Version (NIV)

[6] For the LORD your God will bless you as he has promised, and you will lend to many nations but will borrow from none. You will rule over many nations but none will rule over you.

Deuteronomy 23:14

King James Version (KJV)

[14]For the LORD thy God walketh in the midst of thy camp, to deliver thee, and to give up thine enemies before thee; therefore shall thy camp be holy: that he see no unclean thing in thee, and turn away from thee.

New King James Version (NKJV)

[14] For the LORD your God walks in the midst of your camp, to deliver you and give your enemies over to you; therefore your camp

shall be holy, that He may see no unclean thing among you, and turn away from you.

New International Version (NIV)

[14] For the LORD your God moves about in your camp to protect you and to deliver your enemies to you. Your camp must be holy, so that he will not see among you anything indecent and turn away from you.

Deuteronomy 23:20

King James Version (KJV)

[20]Unto a stranger thou mayest lend upon usury; but unto thy brother thou shalt not lend upon usury: that the LORD thy God may bless thee in all that thou settest thine hand to in the land whither thou goest to possess it.

New King James Version (NKJV)

[20] To a foreigner you may charge interest, but to your brother you shall not charge interest, that the LORD your God may bless you in all to which you set your hand in the land which you are entering to possess.

New International Version (NIV)

[20] You may charge a foreigner interest, but not a fellow Israelite, so that the LORD your God may bless you in everything you put your hand to in the land you are entering to possess.

Deuteronomy 26.1-2

King James Version (KJV)

Deuteronomy 26

[1]And it shall be, when thou art come in unto the land which the LORD thy God giveth thee for an inheritance, and possessest it, and dwellest therein;

[2]That thou shalt take of the first of all the fruit of the earth, which thou shalt bring of thy land that the LORD thy God giveth thee, and shalt put it in a basket, and shalt go unto the place which the LORD thy God shall choose to place his name there.

New King James Version (NKJV)

[1] "And it shall be, when you come into the land which the LORD your God is giving you *as* an inheritance, and you possess it and dwell in it, [2] that you shall take some of the first of all the produce of the ground, which you shall bring from your land that the LORD your God is giving you, and put *it* in a basket and go to the place where the LORD your God chooses to make His name abide.

New International Version (NIV)

Deuteronomy 26

Firstfruits and Tithes

[1] When you have entered the land the LORD your God is giving you as an inheritance and have taken possession of it and settled in it, [2] take some of the firstfruits of all that you produce from the soil of the

land the LORD your God is giving you and put them in a basket. Then go to the place the LORD your God will choose as a dwelling for his Name

Deuteronomy 26.8–10

King James Version (KJV)

[8]And the LORD brought us forth out of Egypt with a mighty hand, and with an outstretched arm, and with great terribleness, and with signs, and with wonders.

[9]And he hath brought us into this place, and hath given us this land, even a land that floweth with milk and honey.

[10]And now, behold, I have brought the firstfruits of the land, which thou, O LORD, hast given me. And thou shalt set it before the LORD thy God, and worship before the LORD thy God.

New King James Version (NKJV)

[8] So the LORD brought us out of Egypt with a mighty hand and with an outstretched arm, with great terror and with signs and wonders. [9] He has brought us to this place and has given us this land, "a land flowing with milk and honey";[a] [10] and now, behold, I have brought the firstfruits of the land which you, O LORD, have given me.'

"Then you shall set it before the LORD your God, and worship before the LORD your God.

New International Version (NIV)

[8] So the LORD brought us out of Egypt with a mighty hand and an outstretched arm, with great terror and with signs and wonders. [9] He brought us to this place and gave us this land, a land flowing with milk and honey; [10] and now I bring the firstfruits of the soil that you, LORD, have given me." Place the basket before the LORD your God and bow down before him.

Deuteronomy 26.18-19

King James Version (KJV)

[18]And the LORD hath avouched thee this day to be his peculiar people, as he hath promised thee, and that thou shouldest keep all his commandments;

[19]And to make thee high above all nations which he hath made, in praise, and in name, and in honour; and that thou mayest be an holy people unto the LORD thy God, as he hath spoken.

New King James Version (NKJV)

[18] Also today the LORD has proclaimed you to be His special people, just as He promised you, that *you* should keep all His commandments, [19] and that He will set you high above all nations which He has made, in praise, in name, and in honor, and that you may be a holy people to the LORD your God, just as He has spoken."

Deuteronomy 26.18-19

New International Version (NIV)

[18] And the LORD has declared this day that you are his people, his treasured possession as he promised, and that you are to keep all his commands. [19] He has declared that he will set you in praise, fame and honor high above all the nations he has made and that you will be a people holy to the LORD your God, as he promised.

Deuteronomy 28.1–13

King James Version (KJV)

Deuteronomy 28

[1]And it shall come to pass, if thou shalt hearken diligently unto the voice of the LORD thy God, to observe and to do all his commandments which I command thee this day, that the LORD thy God will set thee on high above all nations of the earth:

[2]And all these blessings shall come on thee, and overtake thee, if thou shalt hearken unto the voice of the LORD thy God.

[3]Blessed shalt thou be in the city, and blessed shalt thou be in the field.

[4]Blessed shall be the fruit of thy body, and the fruit of thy ground, and the fruit of thy cattle, the increase of thy kine, and the flocks of thy sheep.

[5]Blessed shall be thy basket and thy store.

[6]Blessed shalt thou be when thou comest in, and blessed shalt thou be when thou goest out.

[7]The LORD shall cause thine enemies that rise up against thee to be smitten before thy face: they shall come out against thee one way, and flee before thee seven ways.

[8]The LORD shall command the blessing upon thee in thy storehouses, and in all that thou settest thine hand unto; and he shall bless thee in the land which the LORD thy God giveth thee.

[9]The LORD shall establish thee an holy people unto himself, as he hath sworn unto thee, if thou shalt keep the commandments of the LORD thy God, and walk in his ways.

[10]And all people of the earth shall see that thou art called by the name of the LORD; and they shall be afraid of thee.

[11]And the LORD shall make thee plenteous in goods, in the fruit of thy body, and in the fruit of thy cattle, and in the fruit of thy ground, in the land which the LORD sware unto thy fathers to give thee.

[12]The LORD shall open unto thee his good treasure, the heaven to give the rain unto thy land in his season, and to bless all the work of thine hand: and thou shalt lend unto many nations, and thou shalt not borrow.

[13]And the LORD shall make thee the head, and not the tail; and thou shalt be above only, and thou shalt not be beneath; if that thou hearken unto the commandments of the LORD thy God, which I command thee this day, to observe and to do them:

New King James Version (NKJV)

Blessings on Obedience

[1] "Now it shall come to pass, if you diligently obey the voice of the LORD your God, to observe carefully all His commandments which I command you today, that the LORD your God will set you high above all nations of the earth. [2] And all these blessings shall come upon you and overtake you, because you obey the voice of the LORD your God:

[3] "Blessed *shall* you *be* in the city, and blessed *shall* you *be* in the country.

[4] "Blessed *shall be* the fruit of your body, the produce of your ground and the increase of your herds, the increase of your cattle and the offspring of your flocks.

[5] "Blessed *shall be* your basket and your kneading bowl.

[6] "Blessed *shall* you *be* when you come in, and blessed *shall* you *be* when you go out.

[7] "The LORD will cause your enemies who rise against you to be defeated before your face; they shall come out against you one way and flee before you seven ways.

[8] "The LORD will command the blessing on you in your storehouses and in all to which you set your hand, and He will bless you in the land which the LORD your God is giving you.

[9] "The LORD will establish you as a holy people to Himself, just as He has sworn to you, if you keep the commandments of the LORD

your God and walk in His ways. [10] Then all peoples of the earth shall see that you are called by the name of the LORD, and they shall be afraid of you. [11] And the LORD will grant you plenty of goods, in the fruit of your body, in the increase of your livestock, and in the produce of your ground, in the land of which the LORD swore to your fathers to give you. [12] The LORD will open to you His good treasure, the heavens, to give the rain to your land in its season, and to bless all the work of your hand. You shall lend to many nations, but you shall not borrow. [13] And the LORD will make you the head and not the tail; you shall be above only, and not be beneath, if you heed the commandments of the LORD your God, which I command you today, and are careful to observe *them.*

Deuteronomy 28:1–13

New International Version (NIV)

Blessings for Obedience

[1] If you fully obey the LORD your God and carefully follow all his commands I give you today, the LORD your God will set you high above all the nations on earth. [2] All these blessings will come on you and accompany you if you obey the LORD your God:

[3] You will be blessed in the city and blessed in the country.

[4] The fruit of your womb will be blessed, and the crops of your land and the young of your livestock—the calves of your herds and the lambs of your flocks.

[5] Your basket and your kneading trough will be blessed.

^{6} You will be blessed when you come in and blessed when you go out.

^{7} The LORD will grant that the enemies who rise up against you will be defeated before you. They will come at you from one direction but flee from you in seven.

^{8} The LORD will send a blessing on your barns and on everything you put your hand to. The LORD your God will bless you in the land he is giving you.

^{9} The LORD will establish you as his holy people, as he promised you on oath, if you keep the commands of the LORD your God and walk in obedience to him. ^{10} Then all the peoples on earth will see that you are called by the name of the LORD, and they will fear you. ^{11} The LORD will grant you abundant prosperity—in the fruit of your womb, the young of your livestock and the crops of your ground—in the land he swore to your ancestors to give you.

^{12} The LORD will open the heavens, the storehouse of his bounty, to send rain on your land in season and to bless all the work of your hands. You will lend to many nations but will borrow from none. ^{13} The LORD will make you the head, not the tail. If you pay attention to the commands of the LORD your God that I give you this day and carefully follow them, you will always be at the top, never at the bottom.

Deuteronomy 29:9

King James Version (KJV)

[9]Keep therefore the words of this covenant, and do them, that ye may prosper in all that ye do.

New King James Version (NKJV)

[9] Therefore keep the words of this covenant, and do them, that you may prosper in all that you do.

New International Version (NIV)

[9] Carefully follow the terms of this covenant, so that you may prosper in everything you do.

Deuteronomy 29.29

King James Version (KJV)

[29]The secret things belong unto the LORD our God: but those things which are revealed belong unto us and to our children for ever, that we may do all the words of this law.

New King James Version (NKJV)

[29] "The secret *things belong* to the LORD our God, but those *things which are* revealed *belong* to us and to our children forever, that *we* may do all the words of this law.

New International Version (NIV)

[29] The secret things belong to the LORD our God, but the things revealed belong to us and to our children forever, that we may follow all the words of this law.

Deuteronomy 30:5-6

King James Version (KJV)

[5]And the LORD thy God will bring thee into the land which thy fathers possessed, and thou shalt possess it; and he will do thee good, and multiply thee above thy fathers.

[6]And the LORD thy God will circumcise thine heart, and the heart of thy seed, to love the LORD thy God with all thine heart, and with all thy soul, that thou mayest live.

New King James Version (NKJV)

[5] Then the LORD your God will bring you to the land which your fathers possessed, and you shall possess it. He will prosper you and multiply you more than your fathers. [6] And the LORD your God will circumcise your heart and the heart of your descendants, to love the LORD your God with all your heart and with all your soul, that you may live.

New International Version (NIV)

[5] He will bring you to the land that belonged to your ancestors, and you will take possession of it. He will make you more prosperous and numerous than your ancestors. [6] The LORD your God will circumcise your hearts and the hearts of your descendants, so that you may love him with all your heart and with all your soul, and live.

Deuteronomy 30:8-9

King James Version (KJV)

[8]And thou shalt return and obey the voice of the LORD, and do all his commandments which I command thee this day.

[9]And the LORD thy God will make thee plenteous in every work of thine hand, in the fruit of thy body, and in the fruit of thy cattle, and in the fruit of thy land, for good: for the LORD will again rejoice over thee for good, as he rejoiced over thy fathers:

Deuteronomy 30:8-9

New King James Version (NKJV)

[8] And you will again obey the voice of the LORD and do all His commandments which I command you today. [9] The LORD your God will make you abound in all the work of your hand, in the fruit of your body, in the increase of your livestock, and in the produce of your land for good. For the LORD will again rejoice over you for good as He rejoiced over your fathers,

New International Version (NIV)

[8] You will again obey the LORD and follow all his commands I am giving you today. [9] Then the LORD your God will make you most prosperous in all the work of your hands and in the fruit of your womb, the young of your livestock and the crops of your land. The LORD will again delight in you and make you prosperous, just as he delighted in your ancestors,

Deuteronomy 30:15-16

New King James Version (NKJV)

[15] "See, I have set before you today life and good, death and evil, [16] in that I command you today to love the LORD your God, to walk in His ways, and to keep His commandments, His statutes, and His judgments, that you may live and multiply; and the LORD your God will bless you in the land which you go to possess.

New International Version (NIV)

[15] See, I set before you today life and prosperity, death and destruction. [16] For I command you today to love the LORD your God, to walk in obedience to him, and to keep his commands, decrees and laws; then you will live and increase, and the LORD your God will bless you in the land you are entering to possess.

King James Version (KJV)

[15]See, I have set before thee this day life and good, and death and evil;

[16]In that I command thee this day to love the LORD thy God, to walk in his ways, and to keep his commandments and his statutes and his judgments, that thou mayest live and multiply: and the LORD thy God shall bless thee in the land whither thou goest to possess it.

Deuteronomy 30:19-20

King James Version (KJV)

[19]I call heaven and earth to record this day against you, that I have set before you life and death, blessing and cursing: therefore choose life, that both thou and thy seed may live:

[20]That thou mayest love the LORD thy God, and that thou mayest obey his voice, and that thou mayest cleave unto him: for he is thy life, and the length of thy days: that thou mayest dwell in the land which the LORD sware unto thy fathers, to Abraham, to Isaac, and to Jacob, to give them.

New King James Version (NKJV)

[19] I call heaven and earth as witnesses today against you, *that* I have set before you life and death, blessing and cursing; therefore choose life, that both you and your descendants may live; [20] that you may love the LORD your God, that you may obey His voice, and that you may cling to Him, for He *is* your life and the length of your days; and that you may dwell in the land which the LORD swore to your fathers, to Abraham, Isaac, and Jacob, to give them."

New International Version (NIV)

[19] This day I call the heavens and the earth as witnesses against you that I have set before you life and death, blessings and curses. Now choose life, so that you and your children may live [20] and that you may love the LORD your God, listen to his voice, and hold fast to him. For the LORD is your life, and he will give you many years in the land he swore to give to your fathers, Abraham, Isaac and Jacob.

Deuteronomy 30:6

King James Version (KJV)

[6]And the LORD thy God will circumcise thine heart, and the heart of thy seed, to love the LORD thy God with all thine heart, and with all thy soul, that thou mayest live.

New King James Version (NKJV)

[6] And the LORD your God will circumcise your heart and the heart of your descendants, to love the LORD your God with all your heart and with all your soul, that you may live.

New International Version (NIV)

[6] The LORD your God will circumcise your hearts and the hearts of your descendants, so that you may love him with all your heart and with all your soul, and live.

Deuteronomy 31:8

King James Version (KJV)

[8]And the LORD, he it is that doth go before thee; he will be with thee, he will not fail thee, neither forsake thee: fear not, neither be dismayed.

Deuteronomy 31:8

New King James Version (NKJV)

⁸ And the LORD, He *is* the One who goes before you. He will be with you, He will not leave you nor forsake you; do not fear nor be dismayed."

Deuteronomy 31:8

New International Version (NIV)

⁸ The LORD himself goes before you and will be with you; he will never leave you nor forsake you. Do not be afraid; do not be discouraged."

Deuteronomy 33:13–16

King James Version (KJV)

¹³And of Joseph he said, Blessed of the LORD be his land, for the precious things of heaven, for the dew, and for the deep that coucheth beneath,

¹⁴And for the precious fruits brought forth by the sun, and for the precious things put forth by the moon,

¹⁵And for the chief things of the ancient mountains, and for the precious things of the lasting hills,

¹⁶And for the precious things of the earth and fullness thereof, and for the good will of him that dwelt in the bush: let the blessing come upon the head of Joseph, and upon the top of the head of him that was separated from his brethren.

New King James Version (NKJV)

[13] And of Joseph he said:

"Blessed of the LORD *is* his land,
With the precious things of heaven, with the dew,
And the deep lying beneath,
[14] With the precious fruits of the sun,
With the precious produce of the months,
[15] With the best things of the ancient mountains,
With the precious things of the everlasting hills,
[16] With the precious things of the earth and its fullness,
And the favor of Him who dwelt in the bush.
Let *the blessing* come 'on the head of Joseph,
And on the crown of the head of him *who was* separate from his brothers.'

Deuteronomy 33:13–16

New International Version (NIV)

[13] About Joseph he said:

"May the LORD bless his land
with the precious dew from heaven above
and with the deep waters that lie below;
[14] with the best the sun brings forth
and the finest the moon can yield;
[15] with the choicest gifts of the ancient mountains
and the fruitfulness of the everlasting hills;
[16] with the best gifts of the earth and its fullness
and the favor of him who dwelt in the burning bush.

Let all these rest on the head of Joseph,
  on the brow of the prince among his brothers.

Deuteronomy 33:26

King James Version (KJV)

[26]There is none like unto the God of Jeshurun, who rideth upon the heaven in thy help, and in his excellency on the sky.

New King James Version (NKJV)

[26] "*There is* no one like the God of Jeshurun,
Who rides the heavens to help you,
And in His excellency on the clouds.

New International Version (NIV)

[26] "There is no one like the God of Jeshurun,
  who rides across the heavens to help you
  and on the clouds in his majesty.

Deuteronomy 33:29

King James Version (KJV)

[29]Happy art thou, O Israel: who is like unto thee, O people saved by the LORD, the shield of thy help, and who is the sword of thy excellency! and thine enemies shall be found liars unto thee; and thou shalt tread upon their high places.

New King James Version (NKJV)

²⁹ Happy *are* you, O Israel!
Who *is* like you, a people saved by the LORD,
The shield of your help
And the sword of your majesty!
Your enemies shall submit to you,
And you shall tread down their high places."

New International Version (NIV)

²⁹ Blessed are you, Israel!
Who is like you,
a people saved by the LORD?
He is your shield and helper
and your glorious sword.
Your enemies will cower before you,
and you will tread on their heights."

Joshua 1.3

King James Version (KJV)

³Every place that the sole of your foot shall tread upon, that have I given unto you, as I said unto Moses.

New King James Version (NKJV)

³ Every place that the sole of your foot will tread upon I have given you, as I said to Moses.

New International Version (NIV)

³ I will give you every place where you set your foot, as I promised Moses.

Joshua 1.5

King James Version (KJV)

⁵There shall not any man be able to stand before thee all the days of thy life: as I was with Moses, so I will be with thee: I will not fail thee, nor forsake thee.

New King James Version (NKJV)

⁵ No man shall *be able to* stand before you all the days of your life; as I was with Moses, *so* I will be with you. I will not leave you nor forsake you.

New International Version (NIV)

⁵ No one will be able to stand against you all the days of your life. As I was with Moses, so I will be with you; I will never leave you nor forsake you.

Joshua 1.8

King James Version (KJV)

⁸This book of the law shall not depart out of thy mouth; but thou shalt meditate therein day and night, that thou mayest observe to do according to all that is written therein: for then thou shalt make thy way prosperous, and then thou shalt have good success.

New King James Version (NKJV)

[8] This Book of the Law shall not depart from your mouth, but you shall meditate in it day and night, that you may observe to do according to all that is written in it. For then you will make your way prosperous, and then you will have good success.

New International Version (NIV)

[8] Keep this Book of the Law always on your lips; meditate on it day and night, so that you may be careful to do everything written in it. Then you will be prosperous and successful.

Joshua 1.13

King James Version (KJV)

[13]Remember the word which Moses the servant of the LORD commanded you, saying, The LORD your God hath given you rest, and hath given you this land.

New King James Version (NKJV)

[13] "Remember the word which Moses the servant of the LORD commanded you, saying, 'The LORD your God is giving you rest and is giving you this land.'

New International Version (NIV)

[13] "Remember the command that Moses the servant of the LORD gave you after he said, 'The LORD your God will give you rest by giving you this land.'

Joshua 3:7

King James Version (KJV)

[7]And the LORD said unto Joshua, This day will I begin to magnify thee in the sight of all Israel, that they may know that, as I was with Moses, so I will be with thee.

New King James Version (NKJV)

[7] And the LORD said to Joshua, "This day I will begin to exalt you in the sight of all Israel, that they may know that, as I was with Moses, *so* I will be with you.

New International Version (NIV)

[7] And the LORD said to Joshua, "Today I will begin to exalt you in the eyes of all Israel, so they may know that I am with you as I was with Moses.

Joshua 6:2

King James Version (KJV)

[2]And the LORD said unto Joshua, See, I have given into thine hand Jericho, and the king thereof, and the mighty men of valour.

New King James Version (NKJV)

[2] And the LORD said to Joshua: "See! I have given Jericho into your hand, its king, *and* the mighty men of valor.

New International Version (NIV)

[2] Then the LORD said to Joshua, "See, I have delivered Jericho into your hands, along with its king and its fighting men.

Joshua 6:27

King James Version (KJV)

[27]So the LORD was with Joshua; and his fame was noised throughout all the country.

New King James Version (NKJV)

[27] So the LORD was with Joshua, and his fame spread throughout all the country.

New International Version (NIV)

[27] So the LORD was with Joshua, and his fame spread throughout the land.

Joshua 14:9

King James Version (KJV)

[9]And Moses sware on that day, saying, Surely the land whereon thy feet have trodden shall be thine inheritance, and thy children's forever, because thou hast wholly followed the LORD my God.

New King James Version (NKJV)

[9] So Moses swore on that day, saying, 'Surely the land where your foot has trodden shall be your inheritance and your children's forever, because you have wholly followed the LORD my God.'

New International Version (NIV)

[9] So on that day Moses swore to me, 'The land on which your feet have walked will be your inheritance and that of your children forever, because you have followed the LORD my God wholeheartedly.

Joshua 24.13

King James Version (KJV)

[13] And I have given you a land for which ye did not labour, and cities which ye built not, and ye dwell in them; of the vineyards and oliveyards which ye planted not do ye eat.

New King James Version (NKJV)

[13] I have given you a land for which you did not labor, and cities which you did not build, and you dwell in them; you eat of the vineyards and olive groves which you did not plant.'

New International Version (NIV)

[13] So I gave you a land on which you did not toil and cities you did not build; and you live in them and eat from vineyards and olive groves that you did not plant.'

1 Samuel 3.11

King James Version (KJV)

[11] And the LORD said to Samuel, Behold, I will do a thing in Israel, at which both the ears of every one that heareth it shall tingle.

New King James Version (NKJV)

[11] Then the LORD said to Samuel: "Behold, I will do something in Israel at which both ears of everyone who hears it will tingle.

New International Version (NIV)

[11] And the LORD said to Samuel: "See, I am about to do something in Israel that will make the ears of everyone who hears about it tingle.

2 Samuel 23:5

King James Version (KJV)

[5] Although my house be not so with God; yet he hath made with me an everlasting covenant, ordered in all things, and sure: for this is all my salvation, and all my desire, although he make it not to grow.

New King James Version (NKJV)

[5] "Although my house *is* not so with God,
Yet He has made with me an everlasting covenant,
Ordered in all *things* and secure.
For *this is* all my salvation and all *my* desire;
Will He not make *it* increase?

New International Version (NIV)

[5] "If my house were not right with God,

　surely he would not have made with me an everlasting covenant,

　arranged and secured in every part;

surely he would not bring to fruition my salvation

　and grant me my every desire.

1 Kings 3:13-14

King James Version (KJV)

[13]And I have also given thee that which thou hast not asked, both riches, and honour: so that there shall not be any among the kings like unto thee all thy days.

[14]And if thou wilt walk in my ways, to keep my statutes and my commandments, as thy father David did walk, then I will lengthen thy days.

New King James Version (NKJV)

[13] And I have also given you what you have not asked: both riches and honor, so that there shall not be anyone like you among the kings all your days. [14] So if you walk in My ways, to keep My statutes and My commandments, as your father David walked, then I will lengthen your days."

New International Version (NIV)

[13] Moreover, I will give you what you have not asked for—both wealth and honor—so that in your lifetime you will have no equal among kings. [14] And if you walk in obedience to me and keep my

decrees and commands as David your father did, I will give you a long life."

1 Kings 2.3–4

King James Version (KJV)

[3]And keep the charge of the LORD thy God, to walk in his ways, to keep his statutes, and his commandments, and his judgments, and his testimonies, as it is written in the law of Moses, that thou mayest prosper in all that thou doest, and whithersoever thou turnest thyself.

[4]That the LORD may continue his word which he spake concerning me, saying, If thy children take heed to their way, to walk before me in truth with all their heart and with all their soul, there shall not fail thee (said he) a man on the throne of Israel.

New King James Version (NKJV)

[3] And keep the charge of the LORD your God: to walk in His ways, to keep His statutes, His commandments, His judgments, and His testimonies, as it is written in the Law of Moses, that you may prosper in all that you do and wherever you turn; [4] that the LORD may fulfill His word which He spoke concerning me, saying, 'If your sons take heed to their way, to walk before Me in truth with all their heart and with all their soul,' He said, 'you shall not lack a man on the throne of Israel.'

New International Version (NIV)

³ and observe what the LORD your God requires: Walk in obedience to him, and keep his decrees and commands, his laws and regulations, as written in the Law of Moses. Do this so that you may prosper in all you do and wherever you go ⁴ and that the LORD may keep his promise to me: 'If your descendants watch how they live, and if they walk faithfully before me with all their heart and soul, you will never fail to have a successor on the throne of Israel.'

1 Kings 3:13-14

King James Version (KJV)

[13]And I have also given thee that which thou hast not asked, both riches, and honour: so that there shall not be any among the kings like unto thee all thy days.

[14]And if thou wilt walk in my ways, to keep my statutes and my commandments, as thy father David did walk, then I will lengthen thy days.

New King James Version (NKJV)

[13] And I have also given you what you have not asked: both riches and honor, so that there shall not be anyone like you among the kings all your days. [14] So if you walk in My ways, to keep My statutes and My commandments, as your father David walked, then I will lengthen your days."

New International Version (NIV)

¹³ Moreover, I will give you what you have not asked for—both wealth and honor—so that in your lifetime you will have no equal among kings. ¹⁴ And if you walk in obedience to me and keep my decrees and commands as David your father did, I will give you a long life."

Joshua 1.7

King James Version (KJV)

⁷Only be thou strong and very courageous, that thou mayest observe to do according to all the law, which Moses my servant commanded thee: turn not from it to the right hand or to the left, that thou mayest prosper withersoever thou goest.

New King James Version (NKJV)

⁷ Only be strong and very courageous, that you may observe to do according to all the law which Moses My servant commanded you; do not turn from it to the right hand or to the left, that you may prosper wherever you go.

New International Version (NIV)

⁷ "Be strong and very courageous. Be careful to obey all the law my servant Moses gave you; do not turn from it to the right or to the left, that you may be successful wherever you go.

Joshua 1.8

King James Version (KJV)

[8]This book of the law shall not depart out of thy mouth; but thou shalt meditate therein day and night, that thou mayest observe to do according to all that is written therein: for then thou shalt make thy way prosperous, and then thou shalt have good success.

New King James Version (NKJV)

[8] This Book of the Law shall not depart from your mouth, but you shall meditate in it day and night, that you may observe to do according to all that is written in it. For then you will make your way prosperous, and then you will have good success.

New International Version (NIV)

[8] Keep this Book of the Law always on your lips; meditate on it day and night, so that you may be careful to do everything written in it. Then you will be prosperous and successful.

Joshua 1:9

King James Version (KJV)

[9]Have not I commanded thee? Be strong and of a good courage; be not afraid, neither be thou dismayed: for the LORD thy God is with thee whithersoever thou goest.

Joshua 1:9

New King James Version (NKJV)

[9] Have I not commanded you? Be strong and of good courage; do not be afraid, nor be dismayed, for the LORD your God *is* with you wherever you go."

New International Version (NIV)

[9] Have I not commanded you? Be strong and courageous. Do not be afraid; do not be discouraged, for the LORD your God will be with you wherever you go."

Joshua 10.25

King James Version (KJV)

[25] And Joshua said unto them, Fear not, nor be dismayed, be strong and of good courage: for thus shall the LORD do to all your enemies against whom ye fight.

New King James Version (NKJV)

[25] Then Joshua said to them, "Do not be afraid, nor be dismayed; be strong and of good courage, for thus the LORD will do to all your enemies against whom you fight."

New International Version (NIV)

[25] Joshua said to them, "Do not be afraid; do not be discouraged. Be strong and courageous. This is what the LORD will do to all the enemies you are going to fight."

Joshua 21.44

King James Version (KJV)

[44]And the LORD gave them rest round about, according to all that he sware unto their fathers: and there stood not a man of all their enemies before them; the LORD delivered all their enemies into their hand.

New King James Version (NKJV)

[44] The LORD gave them rest all around, according to all that He had sworn to their fathers. And not a man of all their enemies stood against them; the LORD delivered all their enemies into their hand.

New International Version (NIV)

[44] The LORD gave them rest on every side, just as he had sworn to their ancestors. Not one of their enemies withstood them; the LORD gave all their enemies into their hands.

Joshua 23.10

King James Version (KJV)

[10]One man of you shall chase a thousand: for the LORD your God, he it is that fighteth for you, as he hath promised you.

Joshua 23.10

New King James Version (NKJV)

[10] One man of you shall chase a thousand, for the LORD your God *is* He who fights for you, as He promised you.

New International Version (NIV)

[10] One of you routs a thousand, because the LORD your God fights for you, just as he promised.

Joshua 10:8

King James Version (KJV)

[8] And the LORD said unto Joshua, Fear them not: for I have delivered them into thine hand; there shall not a man of them stand before thee.

New King James Version (NKJV)

[8] And the LORD said to Joshua, "Do not fear them, for I have delivered them into your hand; not a man of them shall stand before you."

New International Version (NIV)

[8] The LORD said to Joshua, "Do not be afraid of them; I have given them into your hand. Not one of them will be able to withstand you."

Joshua 10:25

King James Version (KJV)

[25] And Joshua said unto them, Fear not, nor be dismayed, be strong and of good courage: for thus shall the LORD do to all your enemies against whom ye fight.

New King James Version (NKJV)

²⁵ Then Joshua said to them, "Do not be afraid, nor be dismayed; be strong and of good courage, for thus the LORD will do to all your enemies against whom you fight."

New International Version (NIV)

²⁵ Joshua said to them, "Do not be afraid; do not be discouraged. Be strong and courageous. This is what the LORD will do to all the enemies you are going to fight."

Joshua 18.3

King James Version (KJV)

³And Joshua said unto the children of Israel, How long are ye slack to go to possess the land, which the LORD God of your fathers hath given you?

Joshua 18.3

New King James Version (NKJV)

³ Then Joshua said to the children of Israel: "How long will you neglect to go and possess the land which the LORD God of your fathers has given you?

New International Version (NIV)

³ So Joshua said to the Israelites: "How long will you wait before you begin to take possession of the land that the LORD, the God of your ancestors, has given you?

Joshua 23:10-11

King James Version (KJV)

¹⁰One man of you shall chase a thousand: for the LORD your God, he it is that fighteth for you, as he hath promised you.

¹¹Take good heed therefore unto yourselves, that ye love the LORD your God.

New King James Version (NKJV)

¹⁰ One man of you shall chase a thousand, for the LORD your God *is* He who fights for you, as He promised you. ¹¹ Therefore take careful heed to yourselves, that you love the LORD your God.

New International Version (NIV)

¹⁰ One of you routs a thousand, because the LORD your God fights for you, just as he promised. ¹¹ So be very careful to love the LORD your God.

Joshua 23:14

King James Version (KJV)

¹⁴And, behold, this day I am going the way of all the earth: and ye know in all your hearts and in all your souls, that not one thing hath

failed of all the good things which the LORD your God spake concerning you; all are come to pass unto you, and not one thing hath failed thereof.

New King James Version (NKJV)

[14] "Behold, this day I *am* going the way of all the earth. And you know in all your hearts and in all your souls that not one thing has failed of all the good things which the LORD your God spoke concerning you. All have come to pass for you; not one word of them has failed.

New International Version (NIV)

[14] "Now I am about to go the way of all the earth. You know with all your heart and soul that not one of all the good promises the LORD your God gave you has failed. Every promise has been fulfilled; not one has failed.

Joshua 18:9-10

King James Version (KJV)

[9] And the men went and passed through the land, and described it by cities into seven parts in a book, and came again to Joshua to the host at Shiloh.

[10] And Joshua cast lots for them in Shiloh before the LORD: and there Joshua divided the land unto the children of Israel according to their divisions.

New King James Version (NKJV)

[9] So the men went, passed through the land, and wrote the survey in a book in seven parts by cities; and they came to Joshua at the camp in Shiloh. [10] Then Joshua cast lots for them in Shiloh before the LORD, and there Joshua divided the land to the children of Israel according to their divisions.

New International Version (NIV)

[9] So the men left and went through the land. They wrote its description on a scroll, town by town, in seven parts, and returned to Joshua in the camp at Shiloh. [10] Joshua then cast lots for them in Shiloh in the presence of the LORD, and there he distributed the land to the Israelites according to their tribal divisions.

1 Samuel 12.24

King James Version (KJV)

[24] Only fear the LORD, and serve him in truth with all your heart: for consider how great things he hath done for you.

New King James Version (NKJV)

[24] Only fear the LORD, and serve Him in truth with all your heart; for consider what great things He has done for you.

New International Version (NIV)

[24] But be sure to fear the LORD and serve him faithfully with all your heart; consider what great things he has done for you.

2 Samuel 13.28

King James Version (KJV)

[28]Now Absalom had commanded his servants, saying, Mark ye now when Amnon's heart is merry with wine, and when I say unto you, Smite Amnon; then kill him, fear not: have not I commanded you? be courageous, and be valiant.

New King James Version (NKJV)

[28] Now Absalom had commanded his servants, saying, "Watch now, when Amnon's heart is merry with wine, and when I say to you, 'Strike Amnon!' then kill him. Do not be afraid. Have I not commanded you? Be courageous and valiant."

New International Version (NIV)

[28] Absalom ordered his men, "Listen! When Amnon is in high spirits from drinking wine and I say to you, 'Strike Amnon down,' then kill him. Don't be afraid. Haven't I given you this order? Be strong and brave."

2 Samuel 22:47-51

King James Version (KJV)

[47]The LORD liveth; and blessed be my rock; and exalted be the God of the rock of my salvation.

[48]It is God that avengeth me, and that bringeth down the people under me.

⁴⁹And that bringeth me forth from mine enemies: thou also hast lifted me up on high above them that rose up against me: thou hast delivered me from the violent man.

⁵⁰Therefore I will give thanks unto thee, O LORD, among the heathen, and I will sing praises unto thy name.

⁵¹He is the tower of salvation for his king: and sheweth mercy to his anointed, unto David, and to his seed for evermore.

2 Samuel 22:47-51

New King James Version (NKJV)

⁴⁷ "The LORD lives!
Blessed *be* my Rock!
Let God be exalted,
The Rock of my salvation!
⁴⁸ *It is* God who avenges me,
And subdues the peoples under me;
⁴⁹ He delivers me from my enemies.
You also lift me up above those who rise against me;
You have delivered me from the violent man.
⁵⁰ Therefore I will give thanks to You, O LORD, among the Gentiles,
And sing praises to Your name.

⁵¹ "*He is* the tower of salvation to His king,
And shows mercy to His anointed,
To David and his descendants forevermore."

2 Samuel 22:47-51

New International Version (NIV)

[47] "The LORD lives! Praise be to my Rock!
   Exalted be my God, the Rock, my Savior!
[48] He is the God who avenges me,
   who puts the nations under me,
[49] who sets me free from my enemies.
You exalted me above my foes;
   from a violent man you rescued me.
[50] Therefore I will praise you, LORD, among the nations;
   I will sing the praises of your name.

[51] "He gives his king great victories;
   he shows unfailing kindness to his anointed,
   to David and his descendants forever."

2 Samuel 22.45

King James Version (KJV)

[45]Strangers shall submit themselves unto me: as soon as they hear, they shall be obedient unto me.

New King James Version (NKJV)

[45] The foreigners submit to me;
As soon as they hear, they obey me.

2 Samuel 22.45

New International Version (NIV)

⁴⁵ foreigners cower before me;
    as soon as they hear of me, they obey me.

Psalm 23.1

King James Version (KJV)

Psalm 23

¹The LORD is my shepherd; I shall not want.

Psalm 23.1

New International Version (NIV)

Psalm 23.1

¹ The LORD is my shepherd, I lack nothing.

Psalm 37.25

King James Version (KJV)

²⁵I have been young, and now am old; yet have I not seen the righteous forsaken, nor his seed begging bread.

Psalm 37.25 (New King James Version)

²⁵ I have been young, and *now* am old;
      Yet I have not seen the righteous forsaken,
      Nor his descendants begging bread.

Psalm 37.25

New International Version (NIV)

[25] I was young and now I am old,
yet I have never seen the righteous forsaken
or their children begging bread.

Psalm 34.10

King James Version (KJV)

[10]The young lions do lack, and suffer hunger: but they that seek the LORD shall not want any good thing.

Psalm 34.10 (New King James Version)

[10] The young lions lack and suffer hunger;
    But those who seek the LORD shall not lack any good *thing*.

Psalm 34.10

New International Version (NIV)

[10] The lions may grow weak and hungry,
but those who seek the LORD lack no good thing.

Psalm 37.3–4

King James Version (KJV)

[3]Trust in the LORD, and do good; so shalt thou dwell in the land, and verily thou shalt be fed.

[4]Delight thyself also in the LORD; and he shall give thee the desires of thine heart.

Psalm 37:3-4 (New King James Version)

[3] Trust in the LORD, and do good;
   Dwell in the land, and feed on His faithfulness.
   [4] Delight yourself also in the LORD, And He shall give you the desires of your heart.

Psalm 37:3-4

New International Version (NIV)

[3] Trust in the LORD and do good;
dwell in the land and enjoy safe pasture.
[4] Take delight in the LORD,
and he will give you the desires of your heart.

Psalm 37:18

King James Version (KJV)

[18]The LORD knoweth the days of the upright; and their inheritance shall be for ever.

Psalm 37:18 (New King James Version)

[18] The LORD knows the days of the upright,
   And their inheritance shall be forever.

Psalm 37:18

New International Version (NIV)

[18] The blameless spend their days under the LORD's care,
and their inheritance will endure forever.

Psalm 85.12

King James Version (KJV)

[12]Yea, the LORD shall give that which is good; and our land shall
yield her increase.

Psalm 85.12 (New King James Version)

[12] Yes, the LORD will give *what is* good;
    And our land will yield its increase.

Psalm 85.12

New International Version (NIV)

[12] The LORD will indeed give what is good,
and our land will yield its harvest.

Psalm 84.11

King James Version (KJV)

[11]For the LORD God is a sun and shield: the LORD will give grace
and glory: no good thing will he withhold from them that walk
uprightly.

Psalm 84.11 (New King James Version)

[11] For the LORD God *is* a sun and shield;

The LORD will give grace and glory;

No good *thing* will He withhold

From those who walk uprightly.

Psalm 84.11

New International Version (NIV)

[11] For the LORD God is a sun and shield;

the LORD bestows favor and honor;

no good thing does he withhold

from those whose walk is blameless.

Zechariah 8.13

King James Version (KJV)

[13] And it shall come to pass, that as ye were a curse among the heathen, O house of Judah, and house of Israel; so will I save you, and ye shall be a blessing: fear not, but let your hands be strong.

Zechariah 8.13 (New King James Version)

[13] So I will save you, and you shall be a blessing.

Do not fear,

Let your hands be strong.'

Zechariah 8.13

New International Version (NIV)

¹³ Just as you, Judah and Israel, have been a curse among the nations, so I will save you, and you will be a blessing Do not be afraid, but let your hands be strong."

Zechariah 2.8

King James Version (KJV)

⁸For thus saith the LORD of hosts; After the glory hath he sent me unto the nations which spoiled you: for he that toucheth you toucheth the apple of his eye.

Zechariah 2.8 (New King James Version)

⁸ For thus says the LORD of hosts: "He sent Me after glory, to the nations which plunder you; for he who touches you touches the apple of His eye.

Zechariah 2.8

New International Version (NIV)

⁸ For this is what the LORD Almighty says: "After the Glorious One has sent me against the nations that have plundered you—for whoever touches you touches the apple of his eye—

You must be a child of God to receive his blessings. God reserves his blessings to his children that are faithful and obedient. You too can be a child of God by believing John 3 : 16: for God so loved the world that he gave his only begotten son that whosoever believes in him shall not perish but have eternal life.

Being blessed by God starts with accepting Jesus Christ into your life by being born again.

How to Become Born Again.

If you will like to be a child of God and be a candidate of Heaven by being born again, please say the following prayer.

Dear Lord Jesus, I repent of my sins, I ask you to please forgive me of all I have done against you, wash me clean with your blood that was shed on Calvary, please write my name in the book of life, come into my heart and be my Lord and savior, I accept you today as the Son of God and the only way to Heaven, father please help me to know you more and to keep loving you.

Amen.

About The Author.

Ayodele Awe was called into ministry and charged with revealing the word of God to this generation as relating to the last days. He is the Senior Pastor/founder of House of Prayer for All Nations In Connecticuit an Evangelical outreach Church called to spread the love of Jesus Christ to all mankind. Ayodele is an Evangelist, Pastor and Teacher of the Word of God bringing the message of Repentance back to New England. Pastor Ayodele also features on a TV weekly outreach called Hour of Salvation in CATV6 in Connecticut and other local stations. Ayodele is married to Modupe Awe an Evangelist and Song writer and are both blessed with a son David.